Contents

Acknowledgements

We would like to thank all of the executives who have contributed their hard-won lessons to the Fifty Lessons business library.

We believe that recording the first-hand learning experiences of today's business leaders will prove to be of immeasurable value to the business leaders of the future.

We'd also like to thank all those who have believed in, and contributed their time to, this growing and exciting initiative. Your support has been invaluable.

From the team at Fifty Lessons

About Fifty Lessons

Wherever you are on the career ladder, you are walking in the footsteps of others. Whatever business dilemma you are facing, some of the finest brains in business have faced it before.

Fifty Lessons was born out of a desire to learn from the experience of today's greatest business minds. We felt that decades of hard-won business experience were being written off to the vagaries of memory and resolved to capture, store and pass on this wisdom to the next generation.

Using the power of storytelling, we have captured on film the most valuable and defining experiences of some of the biggest names in international business, and built them into a digital library containing over 400 lessons.

The *Fast Track to Business Excellence* series features specially chosen lessons from this library, offering inspiration, practical help and guidance across a diverse range of management challenges. In business, as in life, learning from the knowledge of others is invaluable. We believe that there is no substitute for experience.

Adam Sodowick

Co-founder

For access to filmed interviews from the entire Fifty Lessons management collection, please visit: www.fiftylessons.com

Introduction to Mastering Change

Change is a fact of life. In business, change is essential for nurturing an innovative, successful and thriving organization, but it can also be disruptive. The challenge is to maintain the process of change while maintaining stability within the organization.

Mastering Change gives you access to the real-life business experience of twelve of today's outstanding business leaders in a pocket-sized format. The leaders' stories provide an insight into winning strategies and a fast track to understanding the process of change.

The collection begins by emphasizing the importance of looking to the future and anticipating change. It also warns of the dangers of delaying change, or allowing sentimentality to cloud commercial reason. Managing, investing in and sometimes losing people are central themes. There are contributions on how the progress of change can be enhanced by effective leadership and the importance of reflecting on previous initiatives within the company. The final chapter reflects on the damaging effects of constant change and highlights that, if change is required, it must be carried out swiftly to be effective.

Whatever your level of management experience, the personal stories featured here provide invaluable knowledge, insight and understanding of how best to master change.

> Future strategies should not be defined by decisions based on past ideas. This backward-looking approach can lead to an out-of-touch strategy going forward.

1

The Future

David Varney

Executive Chairman, *HM Revenue and Customs*; former Chairman, *mmO₂*

My Career

I left university with a degree in chemistry and a track record of inappropriate behaviour in student unions and on the student newspaper. I joined Shell's personnel department before being sent to Australia as Executive Assistant to the Chairman: that is, 'the Chairman's waste-paper basket'. Soon afterwards I was made General Manager in the South Pacific. I returned via Holland to London as Business Development Director to start up a new business in coal. An expansion into global investments followed, and I was appointed Area Coordinator for Australia, New Zealand, the Philippines and Brunei, and was also responsible for marketing in the Far East. I have held roles as Chief Executive in Sweden, Head of Global Marketing for Shell, Head of Refining and Marketing in the UK and later the European business.

I left Shell in 1996 to become Chief Executive for British Gas (then BG), and we took the decisions to split off first Centrica and then Transco from the company, before I retired. I was enticed back to lead the demerger of mmO_2, the provider of mobile communications services, and was appointed Chairman of Business in the Community, the independent business-led charity aiming to improve the impact of business on society.

David Varney

Executive Chairman, *HM Revenue and Customs*; former Chairman, *mmO₂*

If you are not careful, the past just carries you forward; and it carries you forward into a place where the past is irrelevant. The most difficult thing in an organization is really to understand how much of the past you should take forward, and what you should invent for the future.

A few weeks after I joined Shell in 1968, one of the senior managers took me to one side and explained to me what the future would be like. It was a vision based on his experience at Shell over the previous forty years – a period of phenomenal growth. A couple of days later I realized that all the personnel material I'd been presented with was based on projecting the past into the future.

It was a real wake-up call that in big corporations, if you are not careful, the past just carries you forward; and it carries you forward into a place where the past is irrelevant. The most difficult thing in an organization is really to understand how much of the past you should take forward, and what you should invent for the future.

For the previous forty years, the oil industry had enjoyed a period of sustained growth. More and more energy had been consumed; more and more of it was oil. It had replaced coal as the main source of power. Some of us could begin to see a world in which demand would not be as strong as it was at that time. Tactics based on assumptions about maintaining the same levels of growth were not going to lead us to future success – that was one thing. The other thing was that Shell was expanding. We'd gone from having a presence in twenty countries to being in forty, to being in sixty. If you drew the line infinitely, we would have colonized Pluto – and clearly there was nobody there and no demand, so at some point we had to change the way the organization thought.

If you drew the line infinitely, we would have colonized Pluto – and clearly there was nobody there and no demand so at some point we had to change the way the organization thought.

Most of the future is around us today. It's in a lot of the trends that have changed and that we haven't caught up with. In part it's about being aware of what is happening to the demand for your product or your service. It's about testing the assumptions that are built into the everyday culture of the company by asking those who know it best. It's about taking the time to describe to people where the company is believed to be going. Are management's assumptions about the direction in which the company is headed the same as the staff's understanding of where they think they're going?

I like to understand the assumptions in the culture, to understand who the heroes are in the company, what people think the future is going to look like – and how much of that is a repeat of the past. It's important when you talk to people to set out a new view of the future. If you don't, the danger is that your staff will go into the future looking at the past.

I like to understand the assumptions in the culture, to understand who the heroes are in the company, what people think the future is going to look like – and how much of that is a repeat of the past.

If your teams retain attitudes and opinions that were relevant in the past, they become a real barrier to meeting expectations of customers and stakeholders in the future. It's vital to talk about what is going on in the here and now; to explore what is changing and why it is changing.

Ask your team how much, as a company, you truly understand about what customers want and what's causing them to

If you don't set out a new view of the future, the danger is that your staff will go into the future looking at the past.

change their behaviour. Once you open up that sort of dialogue, it's amazing how many people contribute important insights that have value for the company.

Driving a big company by looking only into the past is like driving a fast car around a race circuit looking only in the rear-view mirror. The circuit looks familiar, but it isn't long before you crash.

Executive Timeline David Varney

1968	Degree in chemistry, University of Surrey
1968	**Shell Refining Company**, London
	Joined as a *Personnel Assistant*
	Shell produces and markets oil, natural gas and
	chemicals around the world.
1971	MBA, Manchester University
1971–1974	**Shell International Petroleum Company**
	Responsible for East African area
1974–1977	**Shell Company of Australia**
	Strategic Planning Manager
1977–1979	**Shell International Petroleum**, Maatschappij
	(The Hague)
	European Products Trading Manager
1979–1982	**Shell Coal International**
	Business Development Director
1982	**Shell UK Oil**
	Trading Manager
1983–1987	**Shell International Petroleum Company**
	Area Co-ordinator
1987	**AB Svenska Shell** (Sweden)
	Managing Director
1990	**Shell International Petroleum Company**
	Head of Marketing, Branding and Product Development
1991	**Shell UK**
	Managing Director
	Appointed to the Board. Responsible for Shell UK's
	downstream activities, covering oil marketing,
	distribution, supply, refining and trading.
1996	**Shell International Petroleum Company**
	Director
	Appointed with responsibility for Shell's Oil Products
	business in Europe.

1996	**BG (formerly British Gas)**
	Chief Executive Designate of proposed BG plc
	BG is a global natural gas business.
1997	*Group Chief Executive*
2000	Retired following demerger of Lattice plc (the holding company for Transco), the natural gas transmission system.
2001–2004	**mmO$_2$**
	Chairman
	mmO$_2$ is a leading provider of mobile communications services.
2004–present	**HM Revenue and Customs**
	Executive Chairman
	The new department created from the integration of HM Customs and Excise and the Inland Revenue into a single department.

Business leaders need to be alert to the changing landscape and respond swiftly to changing circumstances – today rather than tomorrow.

2 **Change Today Not Tomorrow**
John Whybrow

Chairman, *Wolseley*

My Career

As far back as I can remember I always wanted to be an engineer – like my father. I took my degree in engineering at Imperial College, London, graduated with a passion to design steam turbines, and joined a steam turbine company called the English Electric Company. After a couple of years I realized that I was finding the company itself more interesting than the technology I was playing with, and that's how I discovered my fascination for business.

After I left English Electric I joined Philips and entered the world of manufacturing. I ran a few of Philips' manufacturing businesses before becoming a Plant Director. A Plant Director is a baron in his own area: all powerful. It was a role with a lot of autonomy, and I was almost able to do just what I wanted. I became very interested in quality improvement, and we were proud to win the British Quality Award in 1985. I then moved into the semi-conductor business and applied some of the things I had learnt about improvement to that business. Then I left Philips.

I had always wanted to be my own boss and was invited to go and run an electronics plc. It was a company in deep trouble. In the middle of turning it around – and we managed to give it a future – Philips asked me to rejoin them. It was the time of the Centurion programme, the worldwide plan to revitalize the company through dramatic restructuring, and Philips was experiencing difficulties: but we succeeded in transforming the business, and Philips survived.

In 1995 I went to Holland to become President of Philips Lighting, and a couple of years later joined the main Board of the organization, assuming responsibility for the medical division, as well as lighting and domestic appliances amongst other things. I kept my passion for improvement and quality; I enjoy the management of change and applying technology to business. I took responsibility at Board level for the leadership of those things – including e-business.

In 2002 I returned to the UK, leaving Philips to develop a wider portfolio of interests. I was subsequently invited to take up several non-executive posts in the UK. I have become Chairman of Wolseley, the plumbing and heating distributor, joined the board of Dixons, the electrical distributor, and became Chairman of CSR, a UK semi-conductor company leading in the bluetooth technology space. My wife has persuaded me to do other things as well, and I'm proud to be Chairman of a nursing home that we're developing.

John Whybrow

Chairman, *Wolseley*

Managers and directors are generally slow to respond to change. We wait for tomorrow. The truth is: we shouldn't wait. We should do it now.

Managers love to talk about managing change. They love to implement change and to encourage others to do so. Managers are not so ready to transform themselves, of course. They tend to be immune to change. It's a matter of 'I'm okay; it's other people who should change!'

We, as managers and Directors, are generally slow to respond to change. We convince ourselves – with the sort of cognitive dissonance that is in all of us – that the situation is not really bad, or that the market will come back. We don't have to do anything now – wait for tomorrow. The truth is: we shouldn't wait for tomorrow. We should do it now.

What drives the need to change? Well, it's an ever-changing world, and we become aware of change from outside our internal business environment. As the external environment changes, we, as managers and directors, need to change our internal business processes to meet our business objectives. The trigger for this may be, for example, a shift of power within an industry sector – in the way that the Japanese came to dominate the electronics sector in the 1980s.

In the early 1980s the electronics industry underwent an international transformation. Japanese companies, such as Sony, Matshusta, Panasonic and Pioneer, became very, very successful; they had developed into very fine companies in electronics, and as a result they basically put most of the American electronics consumer companies out of business. Many US-owned companies went bankrupt, or they were bought by Japanese or Europeans.

At that time I worked for Philips, which was one of the companies under attack: our results became progressively more difficult. That's management-speak for 'things were getting bad'. If the late 1980s were pretty bad, the early 1990s were awful. There was an incident where a profit warning was not given when it should have been, and the President of the company lost his job. Suddenly Philips realized it had to do something. It was a critical moment in the process of change.

If only we'd looked at those issues ten or five years earlier, we wouldn't have had such a dramatic state of affairs to contend with.

Philips could no longer ignore what was going on in the world. The view had always been that the exchange rates would change; or, that because we were Philips and we were big – the biggest in Europe, one of the top three in the world

– we were safe: 'We can handle this sort of thing.' In reality, we couldn't. If only we'd looked at those issues ten or five years earlier, we wouldn't have had such a dramatic state of affairs to contend with.

As a result, 200 managers from across the world got together in a conference room in Holland, and decided that in order to save the situation, we had to make an impact. We had to act decisively to demonstrate that we were taking the situation seriously. Our response was a decision to take out 30 per cent of our population across the world. Just to put that into numbers for you, we're talking about 80,000–90,000 people. And that is what we did.

The world is not going to be recreated in our image; the world will do what it wants to do. We must respond, and respond today not tomorrow.

When you apply such a draconian approach, managers say: 'You can't do that, you can't take out that many staff. The business will die. We can't survive.' The funny thing was, none of the businesses died. Every business survived – and became better and stronger as a result of the change. We improved productivity hugely in circumstances where people had said: 'If we take out that number of people we won't be able to do our jobs properly.' Managers actually protect their own organization during periods of change. In fact, organizations are much more capable than we give them credit for, provided they have good and strong leadership.

The managers at top level resisted that change because they were late in taking action. In the middle, people resisted the change when we decided what to do because they felt it was too dramatic and too severe on the business. However, when we actually forced it to happen, people were amazed at how well the business worked, having made those major changes. Philips was one of only two large electronics companies in Europe to survive that period, the other one being Siemens. It's still a tough business, but, to its credit, Philips is still there.

If only we'd made the necessary changes earlier, there wouldn't have been the need to spill so much blood in order to get back to a good business situation. My message about the management of change, therefore, is that if you see something happening out there that is influencing the marketplace, don't assume that the market will come back to where you want it to be. The world is not going to be recreated in our image; the world will do what it wants to do. We must respond, and respond today, not tomorrow.

Executive Timeline John Whybrow

Mid-1960s	Degree in engineering, Imperial College, London
1968	**English Electric Company**
	The firm had a history in heavy electrical engineering, including aircraft and railway traction. Career started in the year the company was taken over by the General Electric Company.
1970	**Philips**
	Joined the global electronics corporation and was to spend the next twenty-five years with the company.
1987	*Managing Director*
	Responsible for Philips Power Semiconductors and Microwave business.
1993	**Philips Electronics UK**
	Chairman and Managing Director
1995	**Philips Lighting Holding BV**
	President and Chief Executive Officer
	Based in The Netherlands
1997	**Wolseley**
	Non-executive Director
	Appointed to the Board.
	Wolseley is the largest heating and plumbing products distributor in the world.
1998–2002	**Royal Philips Electronics**
	Executive Vice President
	Took main Board responsibility for lighting, medical and domestic appliance divisions, along with leading quality and e-business initiatives within the company.
2002–present	**Wolseley**
	Chairman

> If changes within a business need to be made, don't let sentimentality get in the way.

3a   **Don't Delay Change**

Peter Birch

Chairman, Land Securities Group

My Career

Immediately after leaving school I joined the army; it was at a time when National Service was still the norm. I left school at the end of July, and literally three days later joined up as a private soldier. The basic training in those days was twelve weeks, but after about eight weeks I was tested to see whether I had the right attributes to become an officer cadet. At that stage the Suez crisis broke out, and anybody who didn't pass selection was sent immediately to Suez. Instead, I went to cadet school for sixteen weeks, and at the end of the training course I was expected to rejoin my battalion as a subaltern. However, as a long shot, I applied for the Mauritius Militia, the Jamaica Regiment and the Somaliland Scouts. I was accepted by the Jamaica Regiment. So at the age of eighteen or nineteen, as a subaltern, I was sent out to Jamaica for eighteen months. It was most enjoyable – although there was some rioting in Jamaica at that time, and we had to patrol the streets of Kingston.

I decided not to stay in the army long term, and two years later became a salesman for Nestlé, selling chocolate down the Old Kent Road in southeast London. After about six months I was asked if I'd like to go on a training course in Switzerland, and that's where I met my future wife. They then sent me to Singapore for three years, which is where my wife and I got married. We had our first baby three years later in Kuala Lumpur, Malaysia, where we were still working for Nestlé, and eventually decided we wanted to be based in the UK.

I next joined Gillette, as a Regional Sales Manager. I was posted to Australia as Sales Manager for Australia; then to New Zealand as Chief Executive for the New Zealand business; then to Asia to run Gillette's Asian business from Singapore. There followed a period of ten to twelve years as Managing Director for the UK, Europe, Africa, the Middle East and Eastern Europe.

We were about to move to America for Gillette when I was offered a job in the UK as Chief Executive with Abbey National Building Society as it then was. That was a big change: moving from selling razor blades into the financial services industry was quite an adjustment.

I was Chief Executive for fourteen years. During the first four years it was still a building society, so we worked on a strategy of changing status to a bank. During the following nine years as a bank, we were floated on the Stock Exchange; and I then retired from Abbey National at the age of sixty.

Now I am Chairman of Land Securities, which is the biggest property company in the UK and at number 50 in the FTSE 100 list. I am a Non-executive Director of Trinity Mirror, and was at Rothschild, the investment bank in the City. I also do one or two other things.

Peter Birch

Chairman, *Land Securities Group*

Don't Delay Change

In 1990 I was appointed a Non-executive Director of Argos, the catalogue retailer. It was my first non-executive position and I welcomed it because Argos had several hundred retail networks, and had been highly successful. I was the only Non-executive Director to begin with: we recruited another one. The executors had been there all their working lives, and there had been no changes whatsoever; and the Chief Executive, Dr Mike Smith, had been a great success. He was revered in the City and couldn't put a foot wrong.

All seemed to go well at Argos until Mike Smith began to slow down. He was a heavy smoker and nobody realized at the time that he was ill. He tried to keep going, but unfortunately he had cancer, and it took hold on him. He stopped making decisions; he was seemingly unable to do so.

This situation continued for a couple of years. No decisions were made, and we weren't progressing as we had done previously. As the boss, he was still very much in control. His management team, all of whom had worked for him since the day he'd started, turned out to be yes-men. There was no real debate at Board level, and no desire for change.

As a Non-executive Director, I tried to force change dramatically. I was rude at Board meetings: I made a scene. I also tried the opposite approach – being level-headed – to try to get change through, but Mike was not up to it. He began to miss Board meetings. He didn't want to admit that he had cancer, but eventually he had to take time off work. At about the same time the Financial Director became ill as well, but in spite of their absence they were both still pulling the strings behind the scenes. The City was still supportive of them, and the company Chairman was supportive of them too – but one could see that the business was not going that well.

When there are signs of change in a team and their eye goes off the ball for whatever reason... one needs to effect change and be ready to do so.

At our weakest moment Great Universal Stores (GUS) made an offer for the business. At about the same time the Chief Executive died, and the Financial Director retired on the grounds of ill health. I was appointed interim Chairman. I recruited Stuart Rose as a Chief Executive in order to fight the bid from GUS. (Stuart was eventually to emerge at Arcadia, and more recently at M&S.) We appointed Schroders as our advisors, and we worked very, very hard for the three months that it takes for these things to unfold.

On the last day Argos had 45 per cent of the votes, GUS had 45 per cent and Schroders had 10 per cent. We assumed that because Schroders were acting for us they would give us their votes, but it was the asset management side of the company that owned the 10 per cent. They decided they needed the cash and so sided with GUS. We lost our hard-fought battle.

So what is learnt from an experience like that? One learns that when there are signs of change in a management team and their eye goes off the ball for whatever reason, illness or any other, one needs to effect change and be ready to do so. As a result of not making change, Argos lost its independence. It's a very sad case because everything that Dr Mike Smith had done as Chief Executive had been brilliant. His ideas, in their embryo stage, and the plans that he had put in place, were all picked up by GUS and implemented.

When GUS made the acquisition, some four or five years ago, it was said that the company paid a high price for Argos. In fact, we forced them to pay more than they originally expected. Since then, they've gone from strength to strength, and continue to do outstandingly well. What they have done is to implement changes that we, as an independent Board, knew needed to be made.

If something needs to be changed in the interests of the business, it must be done no matter how nasty it is and how much it may impact on people. Often it is kinder to be hard with people so that they understand the reality of the situation and know where they stand, rather than be soft and let a bad situation get worse.

Spotting and seizing
opportunities that
mark major shifts in
a company's strategy
takes a lot of courage,
but is invaluable to an
organization's progress.

3b   Seize Opportunities

Seize Opportunities

In 1984, having worked for Gillette, the razor blade company, for some twenty years, I was appointed Chief Executive of Abbey National Building Society. Now, one might say: 'What on earth has shaving got to do with finance?' I had worked on the marketing side of the business at Gillette, had no knowledge of the financial world at all, but was employed by Abbey National because it wanted to adopt a strategy of change.

The management at Abbey National realized that the financial services world was going through a period of change, and that building societies were unlikely to have much of a future. Within new legislative guidelines for building societies, there was a minuscule paragraph in a new Building Societies Act that enabled building societies to change status and convert to banks. The commissioner who had written the legislation, a chap called Michael Bridgman, was fairly convinced that building societies wouldn't change because the hurdles he had set were too high.

Abbey National had been a building society for some 140 years and was steeped in the ethos of mutuality. I first approached my Chairman to broach the subject of changing our status a couple of years after I joined the company. It was to take me a further two years to convince both him and the Board that the financial services world was changing, and that building societies needed to change and have more freedom to compete in a rapidly evolving environment.

I directed them towards the bottom line, not just for the sake of the bottom line, but to help them to focus on the issues. We were aiming each year to generate profits, but as a mutual, Abbey National didn't refer to them as profits; they referred to them as surpluses. I remember saying at one of my first meetings: 'What's all this business about surpluses? I thought that's what choirboys wore!' I had to introduce a whole new ethos, to change that image from surplus into something more robust and grown-up, something more appropriate for the modern world.

We eventually went to our shareholders – all *7 million* of them. Seven million customers is an awful lot: we had to get 3.5 million of those members to vote, and 75 per cent of those who voted to vote in favour of demutualizing.

There were no precedents; nobody had done it before; nobody knew what to expect.

These were large hurdles, but we got our message across, and eventually we won the vote and changed status. We became a bank. We were the first building society to convert. Nobody else followed us for four years, so we had a four-year lead in the marketplace. There were no precedents; nobody had done it before; nobody knew what to expect. *We* didn't know what

I directed them towards the bottom line, not just for the sake of the bottom line, but to help them to focus on the issues.

to expect, but after we had become a bank we had a lot of capital. We'd raised over £1 billion from conversion.

We sat on our hands for a couple of years, and then we bought a company called Scottish Mutual. We bought it because it sold life policies. There were changes in the way life assurance could be sold, and we wanted to sell life assurance products through our branch network. It was a hugely successful venture.

We then expanded further. We introduced cheque-books; we went into the treasury business because we had a big balance sheet; we bought a company called First National; we bought a company called Cater Allen, and then another building society, National & Provincial. We bought an ex-building society in Jersey in the Channel Islands; we set up operations in France, Spain and Italy. We expanded. The share price went from £1.30 to £15 in a matter of some seven or eight years. Dividends went up progressively, and Abbey National did well.

What does one learn from that? Well, when we were a building society we realized, and had the foresight to see, that the financial services world was changing, and that we needed to

W hen you see an opportunity in this world it's very important that you grab it because opportunities don't come twice.

adapt and change ourselves. When you see an opportunity in this world it's very important that you grab it because opportunities don't come twice. Do the research and planning thoroughly. Consult one or two colleagues – but don't discuss too widely. Have the courage of your convictions. See the opportunity and act upon it. 99

Executive Timeline Peter Birch

Early years	National Service: commissioned as a Second Lieutenant in the Royal West Kent Regiment, and seconded to the Jamaica Regiment.
1958–1965	**Nestlé** One of the world's largest food companies. Worked in UK, Switzerland, Singapore, Malaysia.
1965–1984	**Gillette** *Regional Sales Manager* A leading manufacturer of blades, razors and shaving products. *Sales Manager* – Australia *Chief Executive* – New Zealand/Asian business, from Singapore. *Managing Director* – Gillette UK Ltd *Group General Manager* – Africa, Middle East and Eastern Europe.
1984–1998	**Abbey National** *Chief Executive* Abbey National is a leading UK mortgage lender and was the first building society to demutualize. (Bought by Santander Central Hispano in 2004.)
1997	**Land Securities Group** *Director* Land Securities Group is the largest property development company in the UK.
1998–present	*Chairman*

When taking on a new role, there is a period in which it is possible to change virtually anything. Make changes immediately and you can always make changes; miss the opportunity and change will be far more difficult.

4

Implement Change Quickly When Taking on a New Role

George Cox

Chairman, *Design Council*; former Director General, *Institute of Directors*

My Career

I think that, like many other people's, my career has been shaped by serendipity and circumstance as much as by planning. When you set out on your career you are unclear as to the direction it might go, and cannot see how the world might change. I spent much of my life in what's now called information technology. There was no such industry when I left university. If I had said I was going into information technology, people would have thought I was going to sell typewriters.

I started my professional life as an Aeronautical Engineer. I spent a couple of years in the aircraft industry, and then thought I'd quite like to move into management. I joined a company that offered a management training programme. However, I'd been there only about a year when the company decided that it needed to 'computerize' its production process. They said: 'George, we'd like you to go into this new computer department.' This was in 1964. I nearly resigned. I thought: 'This is not what I've come here for; I want to be a manager, not a technician.' But I joined the department, and over the next year or so the whole world opened up and the company became probably the most advanced computer user in manufacturing in the UK, if not in Europe. That was tremendous experience – and it was hard at the time for people to get a true sense of the impact of what was happening. We weren't just taking the company's manual records and procedures, and putting them on a computer; we were moving from an environment in which systems never changed into one in which they never stopped changing. This was a sea change in business. At the time we didn't see it because the systems we replaced had been in use since the company started a century earlier.

I moved away from computing, as it was termed in those days, to run a factory for a couple of years; I then thought that I would move into management consultancy for a short period. My intention was to go back into manufacturing and become a Manufacturing Director and head of a big company one day but I wanted to broaden my experience first. So I went to one of the big management consultancies, and, of course, what they seized on was my computer experience. So I led computer teams for some time, before being headhunted by an American consultancy to run its operations in the UK.

This was a defining moment in my career, when circumstances dictated the action. It was clear to those of us in the business that information technology was opening a whole new world which business didn't yet understand. I went to New York to see the head of my new company with plans to develop the business, to meet this major new opportunity – and he wasn't interested. I was disappointed because I was running a very profitable company in the United Kingdom and my track record was good – but he just didn't want to do it. I came back very upset because I thought: 'What a terrific opportunity we're missing here.' I discussed it with a colleague of mine who was running the company in Germany, and he said: 'Why don't we go and do it ourselves?'

I had never thought of running my own company: it had never been one of my ambitions, but it was the only way to pursue my business vision. We recruited other people to join us, and the thing just grew over the years. It included an ongoing membership-based research programme, designed to keep major organizations abreast of developments. When we launched the programme we thought we might get two dozen big corporations subscribing annually. By the time I eventually left the company some years later we had over 500 big corporations around the world sponsoring it. It grew, became international, and took in external shareholders. We eventually floated on the London Stock Exchange, and a year or so later sold it at a very good premium to a big American corporation.

So I went through the whole entrepreneurial bit, and not because I'd ever wanted to be an entrepreneur, not because I'd ever wanted my own name over the door of a company, but because the company I was working for wasn't interested in going with our ideas. I suspect an awful lot of entrepreneurs are like that: they become entrepreneurs not out of financial ambition, but out of frustration.

If you look at the formative parts in my career, they were all opportunities that just came along. I'm not trying to say life is purely luck. You have to make the most of your opportunities and you have to respond to the challenges. You have to do jobs well. But what it has brought home to me is that you can't plan your career. Perhaps you can if you want to become a high court judge or a great surgeon, and you go into a professional vocation like that. Most of us, however, don't know what life's going to be like. We don't know what opportunities are going to be around in ten or fifteen years. All you can do is learn from what you're doing, succeed in the task at hand and seize the opportunity when it comes along.

George Cox

Chairman, *Design Council*; former Director General Institute of Directors

Implement Change Quickly When Taking on a New Role

The importance of making an impact soon after you've taken on a new role was brought home to me by a Director whom I worked for when I was a young man running an engineering factory.

When the new Director took over he'd had only a short period of time with the person he was replacing, so we were taken aback at the first management meeting – on his first Monday morning with the company – when he announced: 'We're going to have a lot of change here; change is needed urgently.' Now, I must admit that this surprised the management team. We didn't think change was that urgent. Sure, things could be improved, but we thought things were progressing quite well. He said: 'One of the things we're going to do immediately is cut the number of meetings. We have far too many meetings.' Well, I suppose we really agreed – but what we didn't expect was his next statement, which was: 'As of today, there are no meetings, other than my management meeting each Monday morning – and a meeting is more than three people in a room at one time.' That was pretty dramatic! And it was clear this wasn't a guideline: it was an instruction.

So I said to him: 'Well, I'm sure that's an interesting move. Of course, it doesn't include the weekly production meeting that I run with all the foremen and chargehands and production chasers?' 'It includes everything,' he replied. Bang. All meetings stopped.

About two or three weeks later I went to him in desperation and said: 'I can't run production unless I can get together with my team at least once a week.' 'All right,' he said. 'How long does this meeting last?' 'Well,' I said, 'it normally starts at 8:00 and goes through to about 11:00.' 'No,' he said, 'it starts at 8:00 and it finishes at 9:30.' 'I'll try,' I said. 'No, no. You won't try,' he replied. 'I'll be there at 9:30, and if it's still going, I'll break it up. Who do you have at it?' I said: 'I have my production control staff, every chargehand and every foreman.' 'No,' he said, 'you can have either the chargehand or the foreman – one or the other.' That was it. And that was the meeting I introduced. It was half the length of time, and it had half the number of people there. And it worked.

A new boss has the power to change almost anything. If you don't use your influence straight away, behaviour will become entrenched again, and it will be much more difficult to change things later.

I spoke to this Factory Director about his shock tactics two or three years later when I was leaving the company. He told me: 'I could have tackled the problem of too many meetings by saying: "Give me a list of meetings and we'll review them." We'd have shaved little bits off here and there. What we did was zero base them. We cut the lot out. I knew that we'd be obliged to reintroduce any really important ones, but we'd

In business today people and companies have to change all the time in order to survive and thrive.

do it on a different basis. It was one of the changes I made immediately I came in because no one knew me, or knew what to expect. If I'd been reasonable, had watched how things were going and waited for several months before starting to make changes, you'd have resisted them. I'd also have been much more accepting by then of the way things were done.' So he did a number of things immediately. He shocked us, and thereafter we knew we were going to get change.

When you take over a role you come into a very fluid situation. Everyone's wondering what the new boss is going to be like. No one knows what to expect. A new boss has the power to change almost anything at that point. If you don't use your influence straight away, behaviour will start to become entrenched again, and it will be much more difficult to change things later.

Sometimes when I've gone into a new role, I've seen the things that need changing immediately. Maybe big changes are not so obvious, and it may not be clear straight away what those changes should be. It's important not to do anything precipitate that might damage the business, so you change some of the smaller things. You make a number of changes that get across to people the fact that things are going to be different. Scrapping meetings wasn't the biggest thing that the Factory Director did, but it sent a signal: 'You're going to run differently; I'm going to manage things differently; we're going to operate to different standards here, and become much tighter.' It wasn't a strategic change, but it was the kind that showed things would be different.

I learnt from that experience, and anywhere I've worked subsequently I've tried to make a point quite early on by changing something – often quite small, sometimes cosmetic – to make it clear that from now on things are going to be different.

In business today people and companies have to change all the time in order to survive and thrive. Creating a business that responds to change, with an environment that is flexible – in which people think and behave flexibly – is vital. It's important always to be pushing every aspect of the business to improve. When you take over a situation you need to get across immediately that things are going to change – and keep on changing.

The message I want to get across to my team is: 'I'm interested in hearing what you've got to say, but basically we're going to do things differently; and what we're going to do immediately is to change this, this, this and this...' That sets the pattern for the future. 99

Executive Timeline George Cox

Early years	Started professional life as an Aeronautical Engineer, and spent two years as a Factory Manager in the precision engineering industry.
1977–1992	**Butler Cox** Formed Butler Cox, an IT consulting and research company. Developed the company and floated it on the London Stock Exchange, before presiding over its sale to Computer Sciences Corporation in 1991.
1992–1994	**PE International** *Chairman* and *Chief Executive* Led the restructuring, refocusing and subsequent sale of this long-established services group.
1995–1999	**Unisys** *Managing Director – Unisys UK* Headed up the transformation of the European arm of the global IT company, from technology manufacturer to systems and services supplier.
	Chairman – Unisys UK
	Chief Executive – Unisys Europe, Services Businesses
1999–2004	**Institute of Directors** *Director General* Instigated major changes at the IoD: membership grew to record levels, as did financial reserves; membership facilities were extended and premises opened in seven cities; the Chartered Director Programme was introduced, the world's first independently accredited qualification in Board-level competence.
2004–present	**Design Council** *Chairman*

In a change process, the most important thing to know is not where you are starting, but where you are headed: and to do that you need a map. But allow time for change to manifest itself, as it won't happen overnight.

5 **Make It Happen**
Lord Sharman

Chairman, *Aegis Group*; former Chairman, *KPMG International*

" I started my career in accounting after I left school. At that time, about 95 per cent of all accountants and solicitors went straight from school into what were essentially apprenticeships. When I qualified, I joined Peat Marwick (later to become KPMG). I spent four years in London, after which I went to Frankfurt in Germany, and spent two years in general practice. I was auditing, undertaking investigations and doing a little bit of tax work. In 1972 I went to The Netherlands and became a Partner, and in 1974 I took over as the Senior Partner. I stayed in The Netherlands until 1981, during which time I ran most of northern Europe for Peat Marwick.

In 1981, back in London, I had various spells in setting up the government practice, the public sector practice, marketing – when the rules on accounting were relaxed – and then became head of the consulting practice both in the UK and worldwide. I followed that appointment by taking over as the Senior Partner of KPMG in London and the south, which was by far the biggest piece of KPMG in the UK. I became Chairman of KPMG in the UK, and then Chairman of KPMG International. I retired in September 1999.

From that point on I embarked on what headhunters call a portfolio career. I also went to the House of Lords. I undertook some government work, including a big investigation into the audit and accountability for the public sector in the twenty-first century. I sit currently as Chairman of Aegis, which is a big independent media group and am Deputy

Non-executive Chairman of Group 4 Securicor, the global network of security operations. I'm on the Boards of Aviva, the insurance company, Reed Elsevier, the publishers, and the BG Group, which is a gas exploration company. I'm on the supervisory board of ABN AMRO, the bank, and I get a lot of satisfaction from being Chairman of the advisory board of Good Corporation, which is a kitemark of corporate social responsibility for small and medium sized companies

Lord Sharman

Chairman, *Aegis Group*; former Chairman, *KPMG International*

The most important thing to know is where you are headed for.

The change process is like any other; it has a beginning, a middle and an end. The most important thing to know is not where you are starting, but where you are headed for; and to do that you need a map. Often people forget about that. They assume that the place where they *think* they are is the place where they actually are – but quite often that is not the case.

Let me give you an example. In any organization you will hear quite a lot of espoused values: 'It's the way we do things around here...'; 'We're good on teamwork'; 'We're long on this, we're long on that...'. When we embarked upon a programme of change at KPMG it seemed to me that we needed to find out what was *really* happening in the organization. What was the reality of how people actually made their way in it? We dug quite deeply into the organization and said: 'Let's find out what it is that makes people do what they are doing. Is it the espoused values? If it is, that's great, because then we'll know where we are, and we will know where we want to be.' In fact, what we found was an almost covert set of values and behaviours. We uncovered this by asking people: 'What advice would you give your best friend if they were joining our organization? What do they absolutely have to do, what must they never do, and what can they get away without doing?'

We compiled the results and called it 'The Hustler's Guide to Progress in KPMG'. When we published it the initial reaction from the top management was that it was ridiculous: 'Of course people don't do that.' As we dug further, it became manifestly apparent that what the people in the organization had said they wanted to happen, and what we said we were doing, was *not* actually what was happening in the organization. As a result, our presumed starting point had to be completely revised. Once we had a new place to start, we had a much clearer idea of where we were going, and we knew what we wanted to achieve because everybody had bought into it. We had a map: it was as simple as that.

Can culture be changed without altering corporate structures? I think it can, and at KPMG I think it was. We went a long way towards it, although not through choice. The imperative was that we didn't have the time to change the structure.

Our organization had the better part of 100,000 people in it, in 147 countries; it is organized as a partnership rather than a corporation. It was therefore going to take forever to sort out the tax ramifications, let alone the corporate structure. It was not a realistic option. The culture of an organization comes from the unwritten things – it's the things that are taken for granted, not the structures.

When you investigate what actually happens in an organization, as opposed to what an organization says happens, it becomes clear that changing culture is about capturing people's mind, capturing their imagination, persuading them to behave in a different way – that's what it's all about.

The only way you can persuade 92,000 employees to adopt a change programme is to convince them that what's on offer is going to be better than what they've got already. The change has to be made attractive, it's got to be achievable, and you must make it appear that it will happen. All these factors are about encouraging people to want to make the changes – because, as always, the most powerful resistance comes not from the people who get up and say: 'I disagree with you'; you can argue with them – that's easy. The most powerful opponents are the ones who sit there and say nothing. The passive resisters are the challenge because you don't know who or where they are. All they are doing is sitting in the meeting saying: 'Yes, OK, fine, yeah, good,' then they go back to their operating base and do nothing. That's the most difficult obstacle of all.

The only way you can persuade 92,000 employees to adopt a change programme is to convince them that what's on offer is going to be better than what they've got already.

The way to confront behaviour that is at odds with what you want to achieve is to embed the new behaviours in the way things happen day to day. For example, we changed all our performance appraisal methods; all our systems were changed so that they focused on the various values we wanted to achieve. In that way, when we were looking at performance, it was discussed and measured in line with our core value areas: clients, performance measurement, knowledge about our people and about the society in which we live. You go back to basics each time. You say: 'How does he or she perform in this area?' Make the changes a part of daily business life: that's the way to do it.

The only reason for change in an organization is to improve the bottom line. I don't believe in altruism in business; I think that's just a myth. The prime drivers for change within KPMG were that we wanted a more intelligent, responsive and flexible organization that would in turn enable us to perform much better in the marketplace. When we perform better in the marketplace, we add to the bottom line; if we add to the bottom line, everybody benefits because it is a partnership.

My belief is that companies can change only from the inside. Companies that invite external consultants to help them with their change process take one of three stances: 'Help me think', 'Help me do', and 'Do for me'. I don't really regard the 'Do for me' category as consulting; it's actually large-scale implementation. You can't put change programmes in the 'Do for me' category because at that point it ceases to be *your* change programme: you don't own your own strategy. The most positive role of the consultant has to be in the 'Help me think' area, and the most important thing in a change programme is that it must be owned, and it must be owned visibly by top management.

In order to signal the change at KPMG, we introduced 360-degree feedback across the company. The feedback on me was published so that everybody in the organization could see it. That's the kind of signal that management needs to give. Amusingly, I took my feedback home and showed my wife, who took one look at it and said: 'How much did you pay for this? I could have told them that for nothing!'

The only reason for change in an organization is to improve the bottom line.

In order to implement the change process, we involved people from right across the organization. We used this atypical approach as another signal for change. The way in which you drive change down to the shop floor is to do things differently. Typically, when new things were introduced at KPMG, a working party would be established. The working party was usually composed of the great and the good: senior people who seemed to have the need to meet in places like Monaco. It was a highly stylized and typical way of introducing new initiatives. When we introduced the programme for change,

Unless top management visibly owns the change process, it is not even worth starting the process.

we put one person in charge of the implementation. That individual was a woman, she wasn't a Partner, and she could work with anybody she wanted. Initially there was a great deal of suspicion about this because we're weren't doing it 'our way', but she worked right through the organization, got right down into the belly of it and won respect.

In summary, I would say first that it took longer than we would like to acknowledge to realize that what was actually happening in the organization wasn't what we *believed* was happening. It took longer than it should have done to figure out that people didn't really believe in the directives that were coming down from top management. Second, we probably went overboard in signalling the process of change. We could have done it more subtly, but as we felt we didn't have a lot of time, we tended to be very direct in the implementation. The great success is, of course, that we did turn the organization around. It is much more flexible than it was in the past, and has continued to prosper. 🙶

1966	**Peat Marwick Mitchell (later KPMG)** *Manager* Worked in a number of overseas offices before being appointed a Partner.
1981	*Partner* – London branch
1987–1990	Responsible for the group's national marketing.
1990–1991	Responsible for operations in London and the southeast.
1991–1994	**KPMG Management Consulting worldwide** *Chairman* One of the world's 'big four' companies in accounting.
1994	**KPMG (UK)** *Senior Partner* Served as a member of the International Executive Committee and on the European Board.
1997–1999	**KPMG International** *Chairman*
1999	**Aegis Group** Appointed to the Board of this independent media group.
1999	Awarded a life peerage.
2000–present	*Chairman*
2003–2004	**Securicor** *Chairman* Securicor was a leading security services company.
2004–present	**Group 4 Securicor** *Deputy Non-executive Chairman* Group 4 Securicor is a leading international security services company created after Group 4 Falck's security business merged with Securicor.

It's important for any organization continually to reappraise the business environment and think about how it might change. Being ready to respond to change with well-developed plans means the organization will move much faster than its competitors.

6 **Monitor Your Business Environment and Anticipate Change**

Paul Skinner

Chairman, *Rio Tinto;*
former Group Managing Director, *Royal Dutch/Shell Group*

My Career

I started life as a graduate lawyer, and then topped up that learning with a degree in business administration. I subsequently joined Shell, which formed the basis of my executive career. I joined them at the age of eighteen because they were helping sponsor my university education, and I retired from Shell aged fifty-eight, so I was with the organization for forty years.

I joined the company because I wanted to lead an international life and I must say I had the good fortune to do just that. Apart from blocks of time in the UK I worked in Greece, Nigeria, New Zealand and Norway, and visited many other countries over the course of my career too.

I started in Shell's chemical business but I also spent time in the other main businesses. Towards the end of my career I took on positions of increasing responsibility in the downstream business of Shell – the global refining and marketing business – which I led for almost five years. Latterly I was also one of the Group Managing Directors responsible for leading the organization globally.

I retired from Shell in 2003 and for the last year or so have been Chairman of Rio Tinto, the global mining company.

Paul Skinner

Chairman, *Rio Tinto*; former Group Managing Director, *Royal Dutch/Shell Group*

It's important for any organization to maintain an appropriate level of external focus by continually scanning the business environment, thinking about changes that might take place in that environment and being ready to respond to them with well-developed plans that are properly executed.

Back in the mid-1980s I was responsible for managing the Shell business in New Zealand. It was at a time when that country was undergoing fundamental economic change and restructuring. For many years New Zealand had been a highly regulated economy, protected by tariffs, with lots of internal rules, regulations and subsidies where appropriate. The country was building up significant levels of foreign debt, and had reached a point where the situation was becoming unsustainable.

It's important for any organization to maintain an appropriate level of external focus.

The new government came into power and decided that it would embark upon a major programme of economic deregulation and change. This led to the rapid dismantling of all these controls, and changed the business environment for many industries in the country in a very significant way.

I was in the oil refining and marketing business in New Zealand at the time, which, like many industries, had been highly regulated. There were prescribed rates of return and margins on different phases of the business: as a major player we were not allowed to own retail outlets, for example. We were operating within a very tightly defined framework that was really quite limiting.

W e'd had in place – well in advance of these changes happening – a contingency plan to deal with the deregulation of our industry.

As the deregulation flowed through the economy all of the constraints disappeared very hurriedly. We *were* allowed to own retail outlets; we could set our own prices; we could invest where we wanted to and reshape our retail network accordingly.

At Shell, we had been thinking about the ramifications of this for a long time. We had been tracking the thoughts and opinions of the different political parties in the country to our industry, and were thinking constantly on a scenario basis of how it *might* change. As a result we'd had in place for some time – well in advance of these changes happening – a contingency plan to deal with the deregulation of our industry. As soon as the political winds started to change direction we were able to activate that plan.

We were able to move much faster than our competitors as the changes came about.

We had already agreed with our shareholders in Europe an appropriate level of funding and were able therefore to strengthen our position significantly in the market as a result of a very rapid roll-out and execution of our deregulation plan. We were able to move much faster than our competitors as the changes came about.

So the major learning from this experience for me was that you'd better keep monitoring the business environment in which you operate; you'd better be ready to reinvent your business as the opportunities arrive, and to execute the changes well. I think we were able to achieve that, but it was dependent on our continuous reappraisal of how the business environment might change.

1963–2003	**Royal Dutch/Shell Group of Companies**
	Joined the organization at the age of eighteen and stayed for forty years.
1966	Chemical business UK, Greece, Nigeria.
1979	**Shell International Trading Company**
	Head of Crude Oil Supply
1981	**Colas Products, Shell UK**
	Managing Director
1984	**Shell Companies**, New Zealand
	Chairman
1987	**A/S Norske Shell**
	Managing Director
1991–1995	**Shell International Trading Company**
	President
1995–1996	Additional responsibility for the shipping business.
1996–1998	Strategy and Business Services, Oil Products
	Director
1998–1999	**Shell Europe Oil Products**
	President
2000–2003	**"Shell" Transport & Trading Company**
	Managing Director
	Royal Dutch/Shell Group of Companies
	Group Managing Director
	Oil Products
	Chief Executive
	Responsible for leading the organization globally.
2003–present	**Rio Tinto plc** and **Rio Tinto Ltd**
	Chairman
	Global mining and minerals company.
	Joined the Board as a Non-executive Director in 2001.

> What really drives people to change their behaviour is being inspired to do so. In times of extreme change, people gravitate naturally towards leaders of conviction, who are able to make sense of the confusion and describe it in simple terms.

7   **Change is Simple**
James Strachan

Chairman, *Audit Commission*, and Chairman, *RNID*

My Career

My career has straddled the private sector, the voluntary sector and the public sector. I have always been deaf, and when I started out after graduating from Cambridge I really wanted to make documentary films. I freelanced for the BBC, but somehow felt I wasn't getting spotted in the canteen quickly enough, so I went into the City to gain some financial independence. I worked first for Chase Manhattan, and then Merrill Lynch for fifteen years. I used to run Merrill Lynch's UK and Dutch investment banking business, but as I got older I really yearned to return to using my more creative side. So I went to the London College of Printing to study photo journalism.

I then became a photographer and a journalist for nearly ten years. It was a lovely life, travelling the world, illustrating travel books and writing for *The Sunday Times*. I suppose I could have gone on doing that for a long time. Sometimes it felt a bit self-indulgent, however, and by chance I met somebody who was involved with the Royal National Institute for Deaf People (RNID) which works on behalf of deaf and hard-of-hearing people in the UK. They said: 'Why on earth aren't you working for us?' So I joined the Board.

One thing led to another, and I agreed to stop doing photography for six months and write them a strategic plan. Then the Chief Executive left and I was persuaded – for a short time – to become Chief Executive myself. It was one of the most fascinating periods of my life: having the ability to change the world for literally millions of people, especially in relation to digital hearing aids and TV subtitles.

I still am involved with RNID as a Board member and now its Chairman, and have also branched out into other parts of the voluntary and public sector. I became a gas and electricity regulator for Ofgem, joined the Board of Save the Children and worked on the National Lottery Community Funds Board. I became more and more interested in the public sector, in how you can actually drive change within it in the same way that we have very successfully driven change at RNID, and before that at Merrill Lynch.

A headhunter phoned me one day and said: 'Would you be interested in thinking about being Chairman of the Audit Commission?' I must admit it was something that really hadn't entered my mind before, but it is an absolutely fascinating job – particularly now when there is a huge public focus on reforming public services in this country, trying to making them more efficient, and trying to make them actually meet the needs of the communities they are there to serve.

That is the story of my working life.

James Strachan

Chairman, *Audit Commission*, and Chairman, *RNID*

Change is Simple

In times of really stressful change... simple, forceful, confident leadership, full of conviction, is gold dust.

Once, when I was advising a major UK conglomerate, I remember being very struck by the Chief Executive telling me with absolute certainty that implementing change was very simple.

He said all you have to do is: first, figure out precisely where you want to go, and be able to paint that Promised Land in Technicolor. Then, ask yourself whether you have the right people around you, particularly at the top; if not, change them tomorrow – literally tomorrow. Third, delegate, but without absolving yourself of responsibility. The buck still stops with you, but you delegate to people to enable them to bring out the best in themselves. Then lastly, you praise their success to high heaven.

That's it. It may seem very simplistic to some people, but actually in times of really stressful change, when you are trying to get people to go over the barricades and go against their natural desire to resist change, this style of simple, forceful, confident leadership, full of conviction, is gold dust.

The lesson I've learned in the public sector, the private sector and the voluntary sector is that effective change is always about leadership, leadership and leadership. If you don't have inspirational leadership, you will never have successful change.

What really drives people to change their behaviour is being *inspired* to do so from the top.

When people observe dominant leadership, particularly dominant leadership that is driving change, they get very exercised by the notion that direction is coming from the top yet it doesn't flow through the organization. There is a tendency to become concerned about 'top-down' command and control, which is a very pejorative concept. However, dominant leadership can also be inspiring leadership. If there is good management in place, it is perfectly possible for direction from the top to cascade all the way through the organization, conveying not only the messages about where the organization wants to go, but also how to get there. Good management inspires people at all levels not just the General at the top making a rousing 'Prince Hal'[1] speech from time to time.

The big thing to understand about change is that it can be very complex. In times of change there is turbulence, a lot of confusion, and a lot of worry and concern. This is all natural – and it explains why, in times of extreme change, people gravitate naturally towards leaders of conviction, who are able to make sense of the confusion and describe it in simple terms; who explain *why* we are doing this, *where* the Promised Land is, *how* we are going to get there, and why the agony is going to be worthwhile. In times of change it is simplicity and conviction that rule.

[1] Reference to the speech made before the Battle of Agincourt by Henry V in Shakespeare's play of the same name.

Executive Timeline James Strachan

	Graduated from Cambridge University
	BBC
	Freelance
1976–1977	**Chase Manhattan**
	Commercial banker
	Chase Manhattan is a world leader in retail banking (now part of JP Morgan, Chase & Co).
1977–1989	**Merrill Lynch**
	Investment banker
	Specialized in public- and private-sector debt and equity financing, and advising governments. Merrill Lynch is a world leader in retail and wholesale banking and brokerage.
	Managing Director
	Became a Board member of Merrill Lynch International.
1989	**London College of Printing**
	Studied photo journalism.
1989–1997	Writer and photographer
1997–2002	**RNID** (Royal National Institute for Deaf People)
	Chief Executive
	The RNID is one of the UK's leading disability charities, working on behalf of deaf and hard-of-hearing people.
2002–present	*Chairman*
2002–present	**Audit Commission**
	Chairman
	The Audit Commission is an independent public body responsible for ensuring that public money is spent economically, efficiently, and effectively.

Change management includes helping people to understand what effect the external environment is having upon the organization and why it is necessary to change. The best people to influence others to change are those who are doing the same sort of work.

8   **Driving Change**
Barbara Stocking

Director, *Oxfam GB*

My Career

I began my career in the United States, having gone there
to do my postgraduate degree, because almost by accident
I got a job at the National Academy of Sciences, looking
at the veterans' administration hospital system. That job
began my career in healthcare, and I worked in this field for
about twenty-five years. I then worked for a period in the UK,
researching the National Health Service (NHS); before working
for the World Health Organization (WHO) in West Africa as
Secretary to a Commission on River Blindness. I then became
a Regional Director and a member of the top management
team of the NHS.

I'd done a lot of work in different countries, but it was only
when I joined Oxfam that I moved away from the health
sphere and began addressing issues such as world trade and
the development of livelihoods in poor countries. That was
really quite a change; nevertheless it built on my experience of
management and working in the voluntary sector.

Barbara Stocking

Director, *Oxfam GB*

Driving Change

I'm interested in how change comes about in organizations. There is a difference between non-contentious change you can just tell people about and insist that they act upon, and those more challenging changes about which you first have to win people's hearts and minds, in order for them to engage with and achieve the change.

Within Oxfam we've recently put in place a number of new management systems, including PeopleSoft® in the finance department and a reporting system for all our overseas programmes. Adhering to these new management systems is mandatory; you can't give people the option of whether to agree or not. There needs to be a clear plan to roll them out and get them working; you then have to insist that people follow the system in order for the organization to work. In the main, people will conform because they understand the benefits and know there are some basic things that you just have to do. However, it may also be necessary to introduce more complex strategies, which often require real personal commitment from your staff, and bringing in ideas from others, in order to succeed.

Within Oxfam at the moment we are asking people to review a number of the country programmes they are working on. Often these are very good programmes, but quite small scale; they are making a difference to the lives of poor people, but in a relatively small area. What we are saying to our teams is: 'You could have a much greater impact on poverty if you spread that change more widely; if you could get other people to copy the model; if you got the government to adopt a policy.'

To do that is actually a big change for all our staff. In part it means helping them to acquire new skills, to be able to think and do things in different ways: to lobby government, for example. The first thing to do is to get them to see the need for the change in approach, and to recognize that it's not going to be a fast process. You have to start from the point of persuading your teams that the change fits in well with their current objectives.

At Oxfam we want to make a greater change and a greater impact on poverty. All our staff would agree with that, so the requirement for change has to be related to the positive difference it's going to make.

You may start by getting people on side with you – but they may not truly understand what you are expecting of them. To achieve fuller understanding you have to work through the organization, sometimes from the top, but sometimes picking people in the middle, ensuring that key individuals

The requirement for change has to be related to the positive difference it's going to make.

It's no good asking people to do more than they understand. To build personal commitment to a change you've got to show first that it can be achieved, and then provide the skills to bring about that change.

grasp the idea, that they want to support and adhere to the process of change, and then really encourage them to get on with it, ideally providing additional support where necessary. By allowing others to demonstrate how the change can happen, by giving people some really positive models who can demonstrate what the change can be all about, you will begin to achieve your organizational change – provided of course that you give your people the skills to achieve it. It's no good asking people to do more than they understand. To build personal commitment to a change you've got to show first that it can be achieved, and then provide the skills to bring about that change.

Our HIV/Aids work provides an interesting example of the ways in which Oxfam is trying to gain greater impact and get people to bring about change. We're not a large medical organization, so we don't deliver lots of drugs and treatment, but in southern Africa, for example, we're working in really destitute communities. At first our people didn't know what to do or how to help. We're working with people to influence their livelihoods – looking at what crops they grow and how they work. Some of our teams started experimenting. The leaders of change, if you like, started thinking: 'We can do this in different ways. We can make livelihoods simpler for people who have got very little energy, or who are looking after sick people.' Really, what we have done is to encourage the people with good ideas to get going and put them into action. The results have given everyone confidence that there is something that Oxfam can contribute.

What we have then said to those first innovators is: 'Now you have achieved that, you can make a much bigger change here.' We are working with them to work with, for instance, the government in Malawi: there we demonstrate the social support systems that are needed to sustain orphan-headed households, or the sorts of changes to crop production that make sense if their population is suffering from low energy levels as a result of HIV/Aids. The changes are about spreading the ideas that we already have. The method works because we've already got models in place that demonstrate success – but also because our people have committed to, and want to make, that greater change.

The biggest difficulty in bringing about change is dealing with all the history. People have been working in a certain way, conforming to a way of thinking or a working model, for a long time. The most difficult challenge is to ensure that we do not devalue the way they have been working, but instead appreciate what they have been doing, and encourage them to say: 'Times have moved on, the organization has moved on, and we can do something different.' Success also depends very much upon who persuades whom to change. The best people to influence others are those who are doing the same sort of work. For example, in the case of our HIV/Aids work, the people who will get others to begin to think differently are the ones who are doing the work now. They trust each other. They know the real problems. Instead of hearing some 'whizzo idea' that those at the top are trying to implement, they are hearing it from their peers – people they know and respect.

The biggest difficulty in bringing about change is dealing with all the history. People have been working in a certain way for a long time.

The key is to mobilize those people in the organization who do want to do something, and who can persuade others to do it. Of course there are always a few who won't go with you, and in a sense you just have to live with that. If it's something really important, you just have to state clearly: 'This is now a performance management issue and you will have to change – or else decide if you want to continue working for the organization.'

The best people to influence other people to change are those who are doing the same sort of work.

No company wants change for change's sake, but in our modern world there is no way that change can be avoided. Change is happening around us all the time. Companies have to change in order to remain competitive. Within Oxfam we are acutely aware that the world is changing. We're living in a world of terror. The locations where we can operate have changed. HIV/Aids is devastating Africa, and we've got to do things differently. We can't stop changing. I think a large part of change management means helping your own people to understand what effect the external environment is having upon the organization and our activities, and why it is necessary to change. Clearly, in order to make the judgements on what needs changing, you have to listen to everybody: you have to listen to outside views and you have to listen to those inside. Then you have to make some pretty fine judgements to decide on the right thing to do.

Some changes are relatively easy to bring about because people in your organization expect to have to conform to them. For example, they would expect to be required to present management information in particular ways, and that the organization should report clearly on finances. There are other changes though where you won't get staff commitment unless people really believe the change is important and will make a difference. These are the changes that take much longer to implement. It's no good embarking on a change management programme thinking you can just roll it out. First of all you have to get people to understand the need for the change and show them it can be done through some of your leading people, in order to get the commitment and to get change spread gradually and deeply.

A large part of change management means helping your own people to understand what effect the external environment is having upon the organization and our activities, and why it is necessary to change.

Change is brought about largely through communication, but also through demonstration. That is the key point. People have got to be able to *see* at least a little of it beginning to happen in order to understand the change that you are trying to bring about.

1972	Graduated from Cambridge University
1974–1979	Master's degree, University of Wisconsin
	National Academy of Sciences, Washington DC
	Staff Associate
	Sussex University
	Research Fellow
1979	**World Health Organization** (WHO)
	Secretary to Commission on River Blindness
	WHO is the United Nations agency that specializes in health issues, encompassing physical, mental health and social well-being.
mid–1980s	**King's Fund Centre for Health Services Development**
	Director
	The King's Fund is an independent charitable foundation, the goal of which is to improve health, especially in London.
	Anglia and Oxford Regional Health Authority
	Chief Executive
late 1990s	**National Health Service**
	Regional Director
2001–2002	**The Modernization Agency**
	Director
	Established in April 2001, the Agency is designed to support the NHS and its partner organizations in the task of modernizing and improving experiences and outcomes for patients.
2002–present	**Oxfam GB**
	Director
	Oxfam GB is an affiliate of Oxfam International, a confederation of 12 organizations working together with over 3000 partners in more than 100 countries to find lasting solutions to poverty, suffering and injustice.

Having an organization that is open to change and reinvention creates an environment where it is easier to call on innovative thinking in times of need. It creates a shared culture, and inspires energy and creative thinking among people when they need to work together to achieve a common goal.

9   **Reinventing an Organization**
    Maurice Levy

Chairman and Chief Executive Officer, *Publicis Groupe*

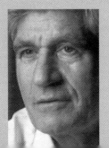

My Career

If I had to give advice to somebody joining an advertising agency, and Publicis in particular, I would probably recommend that the best way to grow is to work passionately, with total commitment for the agency and the client. I was working in another agency before I joined Publicis; I was twenty-nine years old and I was invited by my Chairman for lunch, face to face. He offered me the job of CEO of that agency. I laughed and said: 'I'm twenty-nine years old. CEO? I'm in the wrong agency, because this means that there is nobody here who is better than me.' So I left and I came to Publicis to start all over again with electronic data processing, what today we call IT.

I was fascinated by Publicis; fascinated by Marcel Bleustein-Blanchet, the founder, by his charm, his stories, his powerful personality – and I was lifted by the challenges we were faced with. I always wanted to impress Marcel. In French we say *épater*, which is to make him totally astonished and overwhelmed by the success of an operation. He challenged me to see which level I could work to, instead of building my career in the conventional way by being first an Account Executive, then an Account Supervisor and then Vice-President, etc. The reality is that you are judged by the passion that you put into the work you do, the passion and the commitment that you put into the relations you have with your clients, and how you build the growth of an agency. If you do that right, there is only one way to go, and that is up.

Maurice Levy

Chairman and Chief Executive Officer, *Publicis Groupe*

The best way to adjust to changes in the economy is constantly to reinvent ourselves.

An advertising agency always has to deliver the best possible service to a client, always use the best people and the best tools, and create some of the best ideas and products. Our business is particularly susceptible to changes in the economy. When there is a recession we have to make sure that we can cope with it, and when the economy picks up we must ensure we do not suffer a huge rise in our costs. The best way to adjust to that is constantly to reinvent ourselves.

In 1992 there was a very serious recession in France. Our competitors were faced with having to lay off something like 20 per cent of their people. There were some agencies that had to lay off many more – up to 40 per cent of their staff: as many as 300 people. The impact of losing that number of your staff is huge – especially for an advertising agency. The people who were under threat in our own organization were not responsible for the economic crisis; they were people who had created the corporate wealth in the first place. To lay them off just because there was a recession seemed to us to be unfair, so we tried to create a positive response. We created what we have called the 'economic revolution'.

Every evening for one month all the people in the agency met to try to find solutions to the dilemma. Then we came up with an idea: we held a referendum asking whether staff, starting with the CEO, would be prepared to take a cut in their salaries for a period of two years in order to avoid the lay-offs. People agreed – and it worked. Not only did it work, but after one year we were able to re-establish salaries at their original level.

Never stabilize an organization; never think that its structure is permanent. Encourage instability in order to ensure that you can move boundaries very quickly. Speed and flexibility are needed to create the conditions for reinventing the organization.

By being innovative in the way we managed the structure of the business we not only changed it and managed its survival, but also encouraged innovation in our people. We moved beyond management to create a resource of more energy, more talent, and a culture that is shared by the people. Employees feel good about this company, they feel good about the way we care, and obviously they work harder and more effectively as a result: so at the end of the day we win in every way.

The lesson is never to stabilize an organization; never think that its structure is permanent. Encourage instability in the organization in order to ensure that you can very quickly move the boundaries between departments, between one organization and another, and between one group and another. Speed and flexibility are needed to create the conditions for reinventing the organization. ""

Executive Timeline Maurice Levy

1971	**Publicis**
	Joined what is now one of the world's largest advertising and media services conglomerates, initially to be responsible for data processing and information technology systems.
1973	*Corporate Secretary*
1976	*Managing Director*
1981	**Publicis Conseil**
	Chair and Chief Executive Officer
1986	**Publicis Groupe**
	Vice Chair
1988–present	*Chair* – Management Board

People need to feel involved and respected at all levels in an organization if they are to perform to a high level. Investing in people makes them feel valued and demonstrably improves the whole performance of the business.

Investing in Culture Change
John Roberts

Chief Executive, *United Utilities*

My Career

 I left school with a scholarship from what was then the local area electricity board to read electrical engineering at Liverpool University. I graduated in 1967, went back to the business and worked as an Electrical Engineer. In my mid-twenties I joined the corporate planning unit that was set up for the first time in the business. I'd been there for a few months when I realized that, although I knew about the engineering, I didn't know about the numbers, about the accountancy – and it was actually the accountants who ran the business, not the engineers. I decided that I had to learn something about finance, so I qualified as an Accountant and moved from engineering up through the accountancy department within the organization, becoming Financial Director in 1984. Shortly after that the business was privatized, to evolve into one of the new regional electricity companies that was created in 1990. I became Managing Director in 1991, then Chief Executive in 1992.

In 1995 we were subject to a hostile takeover bid from Scottish Power, which we ultimately lost: and the day after the takeover I was dismissed – the inevitable consequence of losing a takeover bid. After a few months as a freelance, I was asked if I would go and work as an advisor with Welsh Water, which was in the process of launching a bid for South Wales Electricity. In the event, the bid was successful, and I was invited to become the Chief Executive, first of South Wales Electricity under its new ownership, and then, a year later, to put together South Wales Electricity and Welsh Water to form what was then called Hyder Utilities. So for three years I ran this combined water and electricity business. In May 1999 I was asked to be Chief Executive of United Utilities, based in Warrington. That role started on 1 September 1999, and I have occupied it ever since.

John Roberts

Chief Executive, *United Utilities*

Investing in Culture Change

In the early 1990s I was running a newly privatized electricity
company. We were doing reasonably well, but I was conscious
of the fact that we weren't really getting the best out of the
4500 people who worked in the business – a broad mixture
of professionals, white-collar workers and blue-collar workers.
I knew we needed to do two things: enable the business to
perform to a higher standard to give our customers better
quality of service, and cut our costs more and be more
efficient overall.

We decided that we would bring in some outside help and set
about changing the culture of the business because within the
organization we still had a number of characteristics that I felt
were not helping the change process.

We were an engineering-based organization, and a lot of our
managers were engineers; they thought about people in the
way they thought about machines, and couldn't understand
why, if they told people what to do, they just didn't do it. Our
nationalized past meant that we were a very bureaucratic
organization that took a long time to make decisions. The
other concern was that many of our people were very much
process-focused. In other words, as long as they performed
their part of the process, that was all that mattered. Whether
we got the right result or not was not their concern.

The three key issues of engineering ethos, bureaucracy
and the process mindset each needed to be addressed. We

It was a culture that had taken
many years to grow, had taken root
in a very deep way, so change was
not going to happen in five minutes.

decided that we couldn't tackle it on a piecemeal basis, only
at senior management or middle management level: this was
something that pervaded the whole organization. It was a
culture that had taken many years to grow, had taken root in
a very deep way, so change was not going to happen in five
minutes.

Whatever we were going to do, it had to be driven from the
very top of the organization, so my role as Chief Executive
would be to lead this process. We couldn't find any firms
of consultants in the UK that had the expertise to help us,
particularly in the utility area. There were certain things related
to the utility market, particularly the engineering dominance,
that we felt had to be addressed. We eventually found an
organization in the USA that helped us to begin a culture
change process that in the end took nearly three and a half
years. We spent a significant amount of money, but I didn't
regard it as a cost: I regarded it as an investment.

Everybody in the organization went through a process of
learning about how and where we were getting it wrong,
what the problems were, and what obstacles were preventing
people from doing the very best they could. We were not

saying to people: 'You're thinking the wrong way,' or 'Your mindset is wrong'; what we said to them was: 'We recruit very capable people, but because of our culture and inheritance and the way we've organized ourselves, we as an organization are putting obstacles in the way of you realizing your potential.'

We spent a significant amount of money, but I didn't regard it as a cost: I regarded it as an investment.

Most of our managers had been promoted because of their technical expertise rather than their ability to manage people. They had moved into managerial positions but often had difficulty thinking about managing people because they simply hadn't had any management training.

What we needed to do was to develop our managers' understanding of how people work, what makes people work as individuals, what motivates them, what demotivates them, how teams run, how you lead teams, and the dynamics of team leadership. Our approach to helping them revolved around a number of stages.

First, all the managers went through the same culture change process that we were putting everybody in the business through, so this was a shared experience. Then we took all our managers on further training courses, focusing entirely on people management. We also brought in a number of specialists, who worked in teams and taught people about leadership.

We made it an enjoyable experience; it wasn't all hard work. We took a lot of people off site and put them through a number of training exercises. I think what really helped was that they felt the personal benefit, and on returning to the business working environment, they would get positive results almost immediately. It became a self-reinforcing process.

It was their technical expertise, rather than their ability to manage people that had taken our managers forward in the business. We found that they often had difficulty thinking about managing people because they hadn't had any training.

The key lesson was that managing people is very important in any environment, no matter what business you happen to be in. The management of people itself is one of the critical issues, and that needs a lot of focus. Never mind what products you sell or the business you're in: you need to understand those as well, of course, but understanding people is the key to success.

I believe fundamentally that nobody goes to work wanting to do a bad job. It's what happens at work that stops them doing a good job. The whole purpose of the culture change process was to take down those barriers that got in the way of people performing well as individuals and in teams. So everybody went through a process. It started with a three-day workshop to talk through how we behaved, how we interacted at work and how we worked as teams, and we began to explore some of the ways in which we didn't perform as best we could. The importance was, first of all, that it was a learning process from which we all benefited. Second it was a shared experience. It gave us a common language and we began to talk about the issues in the same kind of way. Most important of all, for many of the 4500 people employed by the organization, it was the first training experience for years. The fact that we invested in them was an expression of interest, of belief by the organization that: 'You are worth it. We want to invest in you, we want to help you.' I think that, more than anything else, produced a really positive reaction.

In the space of eighteen months to two years, the whole atmosphere of the place changed tangibly. It became a lot

Never mind the products you sell or the business that you're in… understanding people is the key to success.

more positive, people worked together more effectively, they were more focused on what they were trying to do, and they were more enthusiastic. I go back to my initial diagnosis that we were too process-driven, too bureaucratic, too much dominated by an engineering culture; all of those things changed. We became far more helper orientated; people were asking themselves: 'What is the result here? How can I get the right result?'

They also became a lot more slick commercially: we moved things more rapidly, we made decisions more effectively, and a lot of our middle managers, who were primarily engineers and technologists, became very much more focused on the human side of the business. The lesson for me was: if you invest in people, in their welfare, education and training, and show an interest in them, backed up by a demonstrable investment, the benefits return many, many times over in terms of improvements.

Not everyone will support a change process. Explain clearly why change is needed, and if detractors are still at odds with the company's future direction it is time to part company.

Dealing with Opposition to Culture Change

Dealing with Opposition to Culture Change

I've talked about culture change and stimulating performance: of course, not everybody immediately sees the benefit of that. Not everybody wants to change. The people who are probably most likely to resist in my experience are those in junior and middle management who have some degree of seniority, status or reward; they got that by sticking with the prevailing culture and reward system, and all of a sudden you want to change it. While people at the top of the organization can probably see the bigger picture and understand the need for change, the guys in the middle are thinking to themselves: 'What's in this for me? Why should I change? I've been successful within the existing system and I don't want to trade that in for something else where maybe I won't be as successful.'

One of the big difficulties you have to break through is the permafrost that sits in the organization. You have to address it first by involving everybody, by explaining very clearly – particularly to those people most likely to resist – why you're doing what you're doing, that it's not a threat to them, and in fact will be a benefit. Persuade them to come on the journey with you because it will get better, and they're not being threatened by it.

One has to say that on average, in any organization, about 15 per cent of the people will go with the management whatever they do, and about 15 per cent don't really like the management at all and will be resistant whatever they do.

You're really playing for the 70 per cent in the middle. You move them, plus the malleable 15 per cent, and you've got 85 per cent of the people on your side. There will always be objectors. You have to be realistic. There will always be some people who, whatever you do, don't want to know and don't want to change. Ultimately, with the best will in the world, what you have to say to those people is: 'Look, we're all going in this direction; if you don't want to come with us, fine; you'd better go somewhere else.'

People sometimes think spending money and trying to change performance is just a drain on resources, but in my experience the investment feeds right the way through to the bottom line.

When you've tried everything and people just will not come onside, you have to take decisive action, otherwise they will start to detract from what you're doing with the majority and will be a drag on performance, which is not what you want.

People sometimes think spending money and trying to change performance is just a drain on resources, but in my experience the investment feeds right the way through to the bottom line.

By getting better performance in the business you get better productivity, more cost effectiveness, better top line on sales. If you take away the barriers that inhibit performance, you take away a lot of the friction, the inefficiency, the hidden waste. It's there all the time: people are either working ineffectively, not linking together properly, not working as teams, or engaging in departmental 'turf wars'. I've seen dramatic differences in my own organization as a result of culture change. In the last four years we have developed a small portfolio of businesses focused on external markets that we weren't in before. Three years ago they made no profit. Last year they turned over £1 billion and made £75 million profit. I think those numbers say more than I ever could. 🙶

Executive Timeline John Roberts

1967	Graduated from Liverpool University
1967	**Manweb Plc** Joined the company immediately after graduating. Manweb was a regional electricity company that served northwestern England and north Wales.
1984	*Finance Director*
1991	*Managing Director*
1992–1995	*Chief Executive* Left Manweb following the company's takeover by Scottish Power.
1995	*Freelance consultant*
1996	**South Wales Electricity** *Chief Executive* Was at the helm during its acquisition by Hyder Utilities – the company that provided wastewater services and distribution of electricity and gas in Wales.
1996	**Hyder Utilities** *Director*
1997	*Chief Executive*
1999–present	**United Utilities** *Chief Executive* United Utilities combines water, wastewater, electricity and telecommunications services in the UK.

Change is imperative in business, and it is important to bring new people and fresh thinking into an organization to take it forward – however difficult or unfair it may seem at the time.

11   **Winning Teams Must Change**
Dawn Airey

Managing Director: Sky Networks, *British Sky Broadcasting Group*

My Career

I graduated from Cambridge in 1984 and went straight to Central Television as a graduate trainee. It was an incredible production powerhouse in the 1980s. At the end of my two years' training I started a programming career in light entertainment. I was an Associate Producer on shows such as *Classmates*; a Researcher on *Blockbusters*, *The Price Is Right*, *The $64,000 Question* – all high-quality, long-running entertainment series. What I really wanted to do, though, was to be a Producer in the News and Current Affairs department. My boss used to ask me every six months: 'What do you want to do, Dawn?' I would say: 'I want to be a Producer in the Current Affairs department.' And he would say: 'No, I think you're Entertainment.' He would always give me things to do other than what I really wanted to do. One day he said: 'I think you could be a Scheduler. You're always saying to me: "That's in the wrong place" and "Why on earth did somebody do that?"'

At the time, ITV's schedule was compiled by the big five companies. They got together every other week and carved up the schedule between them. Central Television's planner, a wonderful man called John Terry, was about to retire. I told my boss: 'No, I don't want to be a Scheduler. I want eventually to be a Controller of factual programmes, but a Producer in the short term.' My boss said: 'Well, I'll double your salary, and give you a company car.' The car was the clincher, so I said: 'Fine.' For an XR2, I became a Scheduler of Central for a couple of years, and because I was good at that, I was also asked to run the press office and the presentation department and research. So at the end of the day I was Director of Broadcasting. I was at Central for a total of eight years, but did something new every couple of years.

The ITV Network Centre was established in response to the 1990 Broadcasting Act, which said ITV had to have a separate commissioning and scheduling body. I was recruited as Controller of Children's and Daytime TV. I held the post for two years, and it proved to be a calling card to become Controller of Arts and Entertainment at Channel 4, where I led a team that commissioned everything from *Father Ted* to *Brass Eye*, and acquired *Friends* and *ER*. These were halcyon days, a really fantastic and creative period in Channel 4's history. From Channel 4 I went to Channel 5 – another happy accident.

My career has been a series of happy accidents. I received a phone call from Greg Dyke to say there were four bids going in for Channel 5, and the consortium he was involved in wanted me to be Director of Programmes. I held that post for five years, became Chief Executive for two years, and was then in the lovely position of ITV wanting me to be their Chief Executive. Sky made a very audacious bid on the day I was about to sign for ITV and invited me to become Managing Director of Sky Networks. I thought: 'I don't know much about multi-channel telly, but I need to go to Sky because that is where the bigger challenge is going to be.' And I was right!

Dawn Airey

Managing Director: Sky Networks, *British Sky Broadcasting Group*

Winning Teams Must Change

I believe winning teams must change; it's almost a mantra of mine. I'd been at Channel 5 for five years as Director of Programmes before I was made Chief Executive. I decided I was going to have a crack at doing both jobs for a year, but realized about nine months into the year that it was not sustainable because the workload was too great. So I had to bring in a new Director of Programmes, and attracted a talented individual from Channel 4 called Kevin Lygo, who was then Controller for Arts and Entertainment. The first thing he said after he basically stripped the office bare (because he likes taking a minimalist approach) was: 'I want to change the team.'

Interestingly, Channel 5 had had the same creative team from launch to six years in. The shareholders had always been supportive of the creative team and myself, despite some anxious moments. But the Channel gained momentum and we hit the 5 per cent share within five years. Our share was still growing, we were the most operationally efficient Channel, and the team was extremely talented. Now the new Director of Programmes wanted to change things, which was perfectly understandable. You can't bring in a Creative Director and say: 'Actually, it's all fantastic and you don't need to change a thing.' He *had* to change things.

While you can change the schedule and the commissioning, the most difficult thing is changing the personnel. Kevin said: 'You've actually got a really good team of people here,

but I want to change them; I want to get rid of half of them.'
These were people with whom over six years I had built up
a very close personal relationship. We'd started something
that everyone said would never work, and we'd gone through
an enormous personal and professional journey together.
Kevin was saying in effect: 'I want to get rid of three very, very
dear friends of yours.' These were people who I thought were
superb at what they did. I asked him to reflect on what he
wanted to do and the motivations for doing it, but I knew I
had to let him make changes: and I was right to let him do so
– but it was very painful.

You can't bring in a Creative
Director and say: 'Actually, it's all
fantastic and you don't need to
change a thing.' He *had* to change
things.

It was painful in terms of having to deliver that message to
those individuals, who said: 'All we've ever done is deliver.
Why are we being given a big cheque and told to go and do
something else?' The reason was that we did need to bring
new blood and new thinking into the Channel. Kevin did that,
and he was right to do it. The people he brought in were
clearly very different from those who had left, but added a new
dimension to what we were doing. He continued to focus the
programming on a slightly more serious route, but that made

no difference – things had to change. It was a real shock to the organization because everybody from Tony the security man to myself had been there since day one. Everybody knew that this was the signal of a new phase and some quite fundamental changes in the company.

I actively want people who want my job because they're hungry to do well, and they're going to be bright.

A year later, when I left, half the Directors left as well, and a big turnover of staff started. It was best for the company, without question, because it's gone on to grow and develop on a slightly different trajectory from the way we started it initially; all channels evolve, however, and Five needed that fresh injection of ideas and thinking. Winning teams must change.

But how do you know if a change is right or not? It comes down to a combination of experience and visceral instinct. One of the key things about running an organization is to have confidence in the people around you. I've always had a very deliberate policy of employing the brightest and the best – even if I know that those people may well replace me. I actively want people who want my job because they're hungry to do well, and they're going to be bright.

The way you learn to deal with difficult situations is through experience and through having a boss who is going to allow you to fail sometimes.

The other thing is that you don't have all the answers. I do not pretend or profess to be a guru. I can easily have my mind changed if somebody presents me with a good argument and some interesting evidence that says: 'Dawn, reappraise your thoughts on this.' I'm always open to that, and you have to be. As you grow old, you grow wise, but wisdom is also informed by those people around you, and by experience.

The way you learn to deal with difficult situations is through experience and through having a boss who is going to allow you to fail sometimes. There's nothing wrong with getting things wrong if you understand why you did so, and learn from it. I genuinely believe that every individual in an organization should have an appraisal at least annually, and that individuals should be free to say: 'This is what I want to do.' The organization should make significant efforts to develop staff. That's what I do within my team at Sky. Everybody has a plan for the next few years detailing where they want to go and how the company is going to help them get there; that includes both gaining experience within the organization and being placed in different organizations or sent on training courses.

Where there is resistance to change, and there is always some resistance somewhere, you start by being inclusive and giving all-encompassing explanations of what you're doing and why you're doing it. Then it comes down to: 'Are you with us or not? Because if you're not with us, then actually you're probably in the wrong organization.'

Winning teams need to change because organizations can begin to atrophy around certain sorts of almost institutional behaviour. Teams can become used to working in a certain way, and there's a danger that they'll continue to work that way in the future.

We have entered the digital age. It really is the age of access and connectivity. The world is changing so fast: over the last six years we've gone from having forty television channels to 400, and now broadband is here. *Everything* is changing in this digital world; and, to be frank, if you're in the media and you're not open to change and you're not flexible, you are in the wrong industry.

Companies should change the
dynamics of the leadership teams
probably every five years.

Winning teams need to change because organizations can
begin to atrophy around certain sorts of almost institutional
behaviour. Teams can become used to working in a certain
way, and there's a danger that they'll continue to work that
way in the future. If you're in a fast-moving industry, you
can then find yourself left behind. Change can come from
the influence of particular individuals; it can also come from
outside the organization – when you are forced to change in
response to either a competitive situation or a technological
change.

Internally, companies should change the dynamics of the
leadership teams probably every five years. CEOs should
change every five years, and the management positions
below them should move around. You can still have a career
path within an organization, but you should be constantly
changing, bringing in new ideas, questioning established
practices. You need constantly to refresh the gene pool, and
that actually comes through changing individuals.

Executive Timeline Dawn Airey

1985	**Central TV**
	Management Trainee
	Associate Producer
1986	*Liaison Officer*
1988	*Controller of Programme Planning*
1989	*Director of Programme Planning*
1993	**ITV**
	Controller of Network Children's and Daytime
	Programmes
1994	**Channel 4**
	Controller of Arts and Entertainment
	Responsible for around 50 per cent of the channel's output.
	Channel 4 Television Corporation is a commercially funded television station owned by the UK government.
1996	**Channel 5 (now Five)**
	Director of Programmes
2000–2002	*Chief Executive*
2003—present	**British Sky Broadcasting (BSkyB)**
	Managing Director: Sky Networks
	Responsible for all wholly owned Sky Channels (with the exception of Sky Sports) and for Sky Media (airtime sales).
	BSkyB is the digital provider of pay-TV and joint owner of Freeview.

Change is vital in business, but too much change can lead to confusion and result in 'change fatigue'. Effective change should be implemented in stages.

12   **Change Fatigue**
Gerry Robinson

Non-executive Chairman, *Allied Domecq*

When I left college I had planned to become a priest. Instead, I went along with my mum to Lesney Products and got a job working for Matchbox Toys. I really enjoyed working there. It was a very raw company; I moved around within Matchbox Toys and learnt a great deal. I stayed nine years before moving on to Lex (Transport) Group.

The great thing about Lex was that it was a small company with fantastic ideas about choosing good people, and paying and rewarding them well. At Lex I learnt that if you want something to happen, you have to set out a series of objectives that demonstrate how it can be made to happen. The company was great from that point of view – they employed a lot of very bright, very itchy people.

From Lex I was headhunted to take on the role of Finance Director of Coca-Cola in the UK. Coca-Cola Southern had got itself into quite a mess because it had put another soft drinks company, called Club, together with Coca-Cola. I really enjoyed sorting out the mess. A year later I was offered the great opportunity to become Marketing Director of Coca-Cola – and I threw off my background as 'the finance guy' with great joy. I then became Managing Director of the Coca-Cola operation and I loved it. I had a great, great time.

I then led a buyout of the Compass business from Grand Metropolitan. This was terrific because, in addition to enjoying myself, I made quite a lot of money. It was a good example of how you can change something really quickly if people are behind it – and a lot of us benefited from the reward structure.

Then I became bored. I got bored with the whole catering business. As luck would have it, in 1991 I was approached completely out of the blue to run Granada, the UK-based media and hotel conglomerate. I went along to have a look and I really liked Alex Bernstein (now Lord Bernstein), who was Chairman of Granada, and I had a crack at it. Working in television was a whole new game to me. It was probably the most exciting time in my business career because at Granada there was just so much that I could do, and do very quickly. Along the way I became involved with Sky and ITN; there was a lot happening in both those businesses at the time. Finally, I retired from Granada. Currently I am very much enjoying my role as Non-executive Chairman of Allied Domecq, the international spirits and wine group.

Gerry Robinson

Non-executive Chairman, *Allied Domecq*

Change Fatigue

The secret of management is to understand that for effective change to take place, it needs to happen in a series of steps, rather than as a continuous movement.

People talk a lot about the need for change in business and often change is vital. There are many stories of companies that have failed to change and have collapsed as a result. I've seen the opposite of this too, where managers simply don't want to sit still, where nothing ever lasts, and there is a constant need to keep testing this and checking that.

The problem with having someone with a constant change mentality at the head of a business is that they often underestimate the negative impact that can follow the whole organization bouncing around in a state of constant flux in response to 'today's great idea'.

In such a business, fifteen people might go off and carry out a survey, but by the time they come back the leader has had another four ideas and there are other teams running around pursuing those too. As a result people don't know where they are. The secret of management is to understand that for effective change to take place, it needs to happen in a series of steps, rather than as a continuous movement.

My own experience of this was in Lex Service Group. The Chairman at the time was an absolutely brilliant ideas man, but Lex never really went anywhere because whenever anything started to work he became bored with it and wanted to do something else. The company only became successful when he brought somebody in who actually listened to what he had to say and filtered his ideas, while keeping the company running in a smooth and straightforward way

Effective change is about achieving a balance. It is about acknowledging that change has to happen – but not all the time.

The opportunity to turn around the fortunes of an organization is very exciting, but change must be achieved fast – and carried out only once – to be effective.

The Art of the Turnaround

Never, never, *never* carry out reorganization unless you're absolutely certain you will only need to do it once.

Turning around an organization is probably one of the most exciting things you'll ever get to do because the very fact that it needs turning around means it's in trouble. So the advantage you have in a turnaround is that something has to happen.

It's a simple process: first, you get quickly to the people who run the various parts of whatever it is you've taken over, and you ask them to tell you what the issues are and what they think they're going to do about it. I promise you that within half an hour you will understand who knows what they're doing and who doesn't. More often than not in that situation it's about changing the ones who *don't* know what they're doing because you haven't got much time.

Never, never, *never* carry out reorganization unless you're absolutely certain you will only need to do it once. There's nothing worse than going through some terrible redundancy programme only to have to come back to it again three months later. You've got to look at what the issues are, you're nearly always going to have to change some people and you're probably going to have to take some out of the organization. That's a fact of life. There's no point in having a company going to the floor and everybody losing, so you have to do something about it. Take action quickly and then rally those who are left behind. Be absolutely clear about the changes and make them excited about them. They will be receptive because they will have lived through uncertainty for a long time.

With regard to the people who are going, pay them well. Don't be mean about financial matters and be as generous as you sensibly can, but don't have the people hanging around for six months; get them out.

If you go in to do a turnaround, don't delay action. If you take nine months to do it, people will have just started thinking that nothing is going to happen. They will have settled down again and then 'bang'.

So do it in six weeks – and overdo it. It's amazing how quickly things can start to happen. If you get it right and it starts to work, the feeling's fantastic. People love it. They start to feel confident again, they start to feel that decisions are being made, they know where they are, they feel the mortgage is going to be paid: all of those things contribute to a positive environment.

When I moved into Grand Metropolitan contract services – which was hugely loss making – it didn't take more than two days to pick out the parts of the business contributing most to the loss. Quite simply, I closed three or four of those operations down. In my view, they were organizations in parts of the world that were never going to make any money, yet they'd been allowed to continue operating because nobody had had the courage to say: 'We're going to stop this.' So stopping silly things might sound simple, but it's amazing, particularly in large organizations, how often money is just wasted.

The third step is to look for the three or four areas that really can achieve more. Again, it's surprising how obvious they will be once you start to look at the numbers and talk to people. In Grand Metropolitan contract services, for example, we had one business with 2500 customers. If you get one thing right across 2500 customers it's going to make a hell of a difference, so I spent a lot of time concentrating on that business and reaped the dividends very quickly.

Concentrate ruthlessly on those three things. Really drive them forward, and don't let yourself get caught up in the minutiae of other issues. Once you've got the company on a stable footing, only then can you start to talk about the smaller things, or those that need balancing and checking, but the first step is to stop the nonsense and concentrate on the fast turnaround opportunities. As a good leader you will be able to spot them, especially if you set out to do so at the beginning. 🙰

Executive Timeline Gerry Robinson

1965	**Matchbox Toys**
1974	**Lex (Transport) Group**
1980	**Grand Metropolitan**
	Finance Director – Coca-Cola
	Converted Coca-Cola UK from £7m loss to £17m profit in two years.
1983	**Coca-Cola**
	Managing Director
1987	Led management buyout of Compass (the leading food service company) from Grand Metropolitan.
1991	**Granada Group**
	Chief Executive
1996	Masterminded Forte Hotel takeover.
2000	Merger of Granada Group and Compass Group.
2002–present	**Allied Domecq**
	Non-executive Chairman
2003–2004	Presenter of business series, *I'll Show Them Who's Boss* (BBC TV).
2004	Knighted in the New Year's Honours List.

There is no substitute for experience – learn more from the best minds in business

Did you know that Fifty Lessons has created a must-have digital library containing more than 350 *filmed* business lessons that can be viewed online, from home or in your office?

Through Fifty Lessons you can:

- Experience first-hand the real-life learning of some of the most influential business leaders of our time.
- Gain access to a vast array of concise lessons covering over thirty-five key leadership and management topics.
- Benefit from decades of hard-won learning and experience.

To subscribe to Fifty Lessons, and to take advantage of our special reader discount, please visit www.fiftylessons.com/readeroffer for details.

We also offer customized solutions for larger organizations, from providing lessons on DVD and print to distributing tailored lesson packages via email and corporate intranets. For further information please visit www.fiftylessons.com or

For corporate sales enquiries please contact:

BBC Worldwide Learning
Woodlands
80 Wood Lane
London
W12 0TT
United Kingdom
Tel: +44 (0)20 8433 1641
Fax: +44 (0)20 8433 2916
Email:
corporate.sales @bbc.co.uk

For any other enquiries please contact:

Fifty Lessons
Fitzroy House
11 Chenies Street
London
WC1E 7EY
United Kingdom
Tel: +44 (0)20 7636 4777
Fax: +44 (0)20 7636 4888
Email:
info@fiftylessons.com